Advance Praise for Susan Piver's
THE HARD QUESTIONS FOR AN AUTHENTIC LIFE

"Susan Piver is a deeply intuitive and innovative thinker. She has both tenderness and acuity regarding what concerns us. I could not recommend her more highly."
—Julia Cameron,
author of *The Artist's Way* and *The Vein of Gold*

The Hard Questions for an Authentic Life is a new kind of self-help book, one that teaches you to rely on your own inner wisdom as your guide. It will help you navigate beyond cultural messages about happiness to a genuine and lasting sense of well-being." —Andrew Weil, M.D.,
author of *Spontaneous Healing* and *8 Weeks to Optimum Health*

"Susan gives us vital questions that allow us to listen to what is arising, moment by moment, deep inside our hearts. This listening is the tree from which the fruit of the authentic self grows. Treasure this book of questions, and know yourself profoundly." —Rodney Yee,
author of *Yoga: The Poetry of the Body*

"As Susan Piver shows us in this wonderfully clear guide to living an authentic life, asking a question can be a sacred act—one that creates the opening for wonder, curiosity, and genuine response from the true self. This slender but profound book has humility and compassion that broadcasts its deep truths—let it steer you wisely and well." —Belleruth Naparstek,
author of *Your Sixth Sense* and creator of the
Health Journeys audio series

"I'm a firm advocate of a set of checklists to keep our lives clear and focused in the right direction, and Susan Piver delivers an elegant one for tuning in on ourselves and how we're doing in the game called life."
—David Allen,
author of *Getting Things Done: the Art of Stress-Free Productivity* and
Ready for Anything: 52 Productivity Principles for Work and Life

"Susan Piver exudes the joy of a person living from her authentic self. Read *The Hard Questions for an Authentic Life* and learn from her."
—Judith Orloff, M.D.,
author of *Positive Energy* and *Intuitive Healing*

"Too many popular books promise to give us answers. But what we get is someone else's opinions and insights. Only we can find the answers to life's truly important questions. Susan Piver's book gives us the inestimable gift of asking us the right questions—the hard questions...the questions that guide us beneath the surface...to access soul...to find authentic life."
—Robert Gass,
author of *Chanting: Discovering Spirit in Sound*,
composer, and founder of Spring Hill Music

"*The Hard Questions for an Authentic Life* is a little jewel of a book. Open it and dive into the questions. Be warned, however, that your life will profoundly change once you begin this magical journey within. Take it page by page, question by question and unfold into who you were meant to be! Good luck!"
—Mimi Doe,
founder of SpiritualParenting.com and author of
Busy but Balanced and *10 Principles for Spiritual Parenting*

"Susan Piver is a magician, bringing to life a world of healing for all her readers. She rightfully takes her place in the healing world with her keen vision and compassionate heart. *The Hard Questions* delivers accessible opportunities for healing and awakening right to our front door."
—Mark A. Hyman M.D.,
medical director, Canyon Ranch in the Berkshires,
author of *Ultraprevention: The 6-Week Plan that Will Make You Healthy for Life*

"You don't just read Susan Piver's *The Hard Questions for an Authentic Life*, you experience it. Her questions will resonate with anyone who seeks balance, purpose, and joy in life. Each question is a beautifully crafted and compassionate wake-up call to being present and aware of our essential selves and of the glorious reality we are all capable of living, moment by moment. If you buy only one book for yourself this season, make it this one."
—Celia Straus,
author of *Prayers on My Pillow* and *The Mother Daughter Circle*

THE HARD Questions
for an Authentic Life

100 ESSENTIAL QUESTIONS

FOR DESIGNING YOUR LIFE

FROM THE INSIDE OUT

THE HARD Questions

for an Authentic Life

Susan Piver

GOTHAM BOOKS

GOTHAM BOOKS
Published by Penguin Group (USA) Inc.
375 Hudson Street, New York, New York 10014, U.S.A.
Penguin Books Ltd, Registered Offices: 80 Strand, London WC2R 0RL, England
Penguin Books Australia Ltd, 250 Camberwell Road, Camberwell, Victoria 3124, Australia
Penguin Books Canada Ltd, 10 Alcorn Avenue, Toronto, Ontario, Canada M4V 3B2
Penguin Books (NZ) Ltd, Cnr Rosedale and Airborne Roads,
Albany, Auckland 1310, New Zealand

Published by Gotham Books, a division of Penguin Group (USA) Inc.

First printing, January 2004
10   9   8   7   6   5   4   3   2   1

Grateful acknowledgment is made for permission to reprint the following:
An excerpt from "Little Gidding" in FOUR QUARTETS by T.S. Eliot, published by
Faber and Faber Ltd., copyright © 1942 by T.S. Eliot, renewed 1970 by Esme Valerie Eliot.
Reprinted by permission of Harcourt, Inc.

Gotham Books and the skyscraper logo are trademarks of Penguin Group (USA) Inc.

LIBRARY OF CONGRESS CATALOGING-IN-PUBLICATION DATA

Piver, Susan, 1957–
The hard questions for an authentic life : 100 essential questions
for designing your life from the inside out / Susan Piver.
p. cm.
ISBN 1-592-40042-6 (alk. paper)
1. Life.   2. Conduct of life.   3. Authenticity (Philosophy).   I. Title.
BD431.P57 2004
170'.44—dc22
2003019230

Printed in the United States of America
Set in Weiss
Designed by Jaye Zimet

To Josh Baran, for the gift of his friendship here and now
To Michael Carroll, for being a steadfast and skillful dharma brother
To Duncan H. Browne III, for his authentic love

ACKNOWLEDGMENTS

Sincere thanks and a deep bow to Lori Andiman, Richard Borofsky, Robert Bosnak, Duncan H. Browne IV, Joel Fotinos, Amy Fox, Debra Goldstein, Beth Grossman, Joel Heller, Judith Kern, Lauren Marino, William McKeever, Erin Moore, David Nichtern, Derek O'Brien, all the Pivers, Judith Putman-Sette, Jill Satterfield, William Shinker, Ken Siman, Hilary Terrell, Tulku Thondup, Lila Wheeler.

Special thanks to Richard Pine for his creativity and vision.

If you call forth that which is in you, it will save you.
If you do not call forth what is in you, it will destroy you.
—Gospel of St. Thomas

CONTENTS

INTRODUCTION

The search for authenticity is among our deepest and most natural inclinations. Anyone can live an authentic life. Living authentically doesn't require you to secure your dream job, get in perfect shape, or find true love. Certainly those are wonderful, but there is no guarantee that reaching any of these goals will provide the sense of confidence, joy, and ease that comes with authenticity. Haven't you known people who seem to "have it all," yet are not content? Hasn't each of us had the experience of finally securing something—the job, the boyfriend, the home, the perfect weight— that we've always longed for, thinking that this, at last, will mark the beginning of "real" life? I know I have. I also know that every time I find something I've been searching for . . . nothing happens. Invariably, after the first rush of happiness, I find myself wanting something more, again, imagining that my "real" life is just around the next corner.

While living an authentic life might include meaningful work, great relationships, health and beauty, and a great house, none of these has the power to unmask your true self, or settle you in the center of the life you are meant to live.

What does it mean to live authentically? Living authentically is what you're doing when you find congruence between your inner world—your feelings, values, gifts, needs, spirituality, and passions—and your outer world—your job, relationships, home, and community. When you live your authentic life, these things support and synergize each other. It doesn't mean that you have no worries, conflicts, or fears; you may even have more as you choose to live authentically. There is one key difference, though: they no longer have the power to unseat you. When you have discovered what you can offer to others, when you feel that you are on your unique path, when you have an on-going, honest, reliable connection to your inner wisdom, then you have found your unique spot in this world with all its craziness, sorrow, and joy. This discovery gives tremendous ease. You finally have a way of relating to work, lovers, friends, and spiritual practices with open-heartedness and intelligence. Problems, no matter how intense, are workable.

When I was a small child, I used to lie in bed and wonder where my real life was and when it would begin. I would sniff the suburban air, tune into the sound of the occasional car in the distance, look at the lovely, manicured lawns out the window, and try to locate anything at all that felt, sounded, or smelled right to me. Nothing did.

For whatever reason, my early life, peaceful and secure as it was, didn't feel comfortable. I had the distinct sense that I didn't fit in—at home, at play, at school. I wasn't academically talented or good at making friends. The things I was interested in didn't appeal to anyone else. What I was good at—writing, reading, wondering about why people acted the way they did—didn't elicit much response. I felt isolated.

I always felt that my "real" life lay elsewhere. Even then, I knew (or hoped) that somewhere there were people who explored the worlds around and within them, engaged in passionate relationships, lived purposeful lives, and even connected with God. I believed that these were the qualities that made life worth living and that my life, once I located it, would connect me to them. I would find the joy of true love. I would discover my unique gifts. I would engage in work that allowed me to offer those gifts with courage and dignity. I would know God, the Goddess, Jesus, and the Buddha. I would come to a deep understanding of what it meant to be human and, specifically, what it meant to be Susan Piver. This understanding would naturally lead me to my true place in this life.

But where was it?

Interactions with family members did not yield many clues. School was the antithesis of it. Occasional friendships gave a taste of meaningful connection. I found the best clues in music, books, and movies. These gave valuable but often confusing pictures of what "it" might look and feel like. But when I turned off the radio, closed the book, or left the theater, I came back to a diminished world.

I knew I didn't want to live a compromised life, one in which the inner life and outer life were mismatched, where my values, talents, and thoughts were uncalled for in my work, relationships, and community. Throughout my life—and I know I'm not alone in this—I have been accompanied by a powerful wish to live fully, to throw myself on the fire of my own life—once I knew what it was. *Tell me what I should do with my life and I will give everything to it.* This thought has driven me from job to job, from town to town, from relationship to relationship. It seemed clear that the only way to figure out what to do with my life was to figure out who I was. Early in my life I made a commitment to do just this. I used to prowl around bookstores, praying for a book that could walk me through the steps needed to calculate the answer.

I believe that this longing to find one's place is among the most primary of human urges. Once basic needs are satisfied, our minds naturally turn to questions of meaning. "Who am I?" "Why am I here?" "What are my special gifts?" These questions are so basic, so gut level, yet they are profoundly difficult to answer. Why would you trust anyone else to answer them for you? Who better to answer these questions than the only person who has ever lived your life from the inside out, who knows the subtleties of your heart's pains and pleasures? Who better than the only person who will ever be able to accurately tally every last moment of your life, underscore the column, and total the result? The inventory of your existence—thoughts, emotions, insights, sensations—is available to only you. Yet, often, the last place we look when trying to answer life's hard questions is within.

For a long time, I believed that I could live an authentic life by making up a blueprint for action that encompassed my goals and objectives. I spent many hours visualizing, planning, and writing out elaborate plans. But strange things kept happening. My goals kept changing. My personality and values continually evolved. I would reach a desired outcome only to find it was different than I had anticipated. I would fail to achieve my purpose, and something cool would happen anyway. What I thought would bring me pleasure often did not. What I imagined would be painful was not as bad—or was worse—than anticipated. Things kept intruding on my plans: Relationships came and went. Skills that I had counted on became unreliable as external circumstances altered. Unknown talents surfaced to meet new challenges. Opportunities materialized and fell away. True love felt one way, then another. My big questions about life were never answered; I just started caring about new questions. I realized that my authentic life couldn't be achieved by imagining the perfect scenario and then trying to create it. It simply never worked out that way.

After working through failed plans, unplanned successes, new interests, deepening values, and shifting relationships—I realized something important about living authentically: I couldn't count on my thoughts and ideas about what would make me happy *to make me happy*. So I stopped planning. I stopped imagining a career path. I stopped trying to figure out what city I would be happiest living in. I stopped thinking I had a "type" when it came to intimate relationships. I stopped envisioning the house I would live in. All this ever did was create confusion in my life. It was only by cultivating the ability to be present to what was actually occurring, to how I was feeling, to the feelings of those around me, to my relationships *today*, my job *today*, my body *today* that I ever achieved a measure of clarity and direction. Something really interesting began occurring when I adopted this stance: I had more accurate insights about myself, my relationships, and the events of my life. I made better decisions about where and with whom to invest my time, energy, abilities, and feelings. My intuition got stronger and stronger. My ability to listen to myself kept deepening. At some point, after giving up on figuring out what my life's purpose was . . . I noticed that I was living it instead. I was choosing relationships that nurtured my inner life. I was working on projects I valued with people I treasured. The gifts that I had to give were required to execute my responsibilities. My creativity was blossoming. I was living an authentic life. At last.

What I found was that as I was able to fully live each moment, an authentic life naturally and directly arose around me. This life was not created by my thoughts or directed by my will, but was manifested through an ongoing dialogue within myself and with the world, a dialogue based on inquiry and a commitment to listen to the answers that arose. I've come to the realization that it's actually impossible to plan an authentic life—it's only possible to *be* authentic and watch as your authentic life manifests around you.

We live in a society that declines to teach us how to be authentic, how to wake up to our own inner lives. Our own being, that with which we are most intimate, is also, for many of us, the thing that is most inscrutable to us. For most of human history, tending to basic needs precluded all but the most privileged from wondering what their life path might be. For the majority, when moments of contemplation did lead to questioning, answers were offered by religious or spiritual doctrine.

An unprecedented number of us are now looking for our own answers to life's hard questions. We are no longer satisfied with the vision for life offered by clergy, family, society. We can no longer look to outside sources or institutions, no matter how cherished, to hand us a working vision of how to become an adult, find a spouse, raise children, or engage in meaningful work. It is up to each of us, individually and with those closest to us, to discover our own personal vision of life. How amazing: in our lifetime, the locus of responsibility for choosing a path has shifted away from religion, culture, society to . . . ourselves. Yet we've received virtually no education or training for assuming this potent task.

It's no wonder that in the last twenty-five years or so, an overwhelming quantity of personal growth books, workshops, therapies, seminars, and theories have been created. Spiritual trends cycle through faster and faster; even powerful wisdom traditions such as Christian mysticism, Buddhism, yoga, kabbalah, and shamanism are in danger of losing their potency through the speed with which we try them on and discard them. An enormous existential, spiritual gap has been created and we have looked to fill it from all external sources, doing anything to postpone the difficulty of looking within and working with what is found there, realizing that there is no guide, no teacher, no expert, and no other individual who can know how we should live our lives. If we truly want to discover the purpose of our lives, be guided by our own inner wisdom, and live with authenticity, this—assuming primary responsibility for our own precious human life—is the most important shift we can ever make.

Our culture discourages this shift by offering to life's hard questions a plethora of attractive, convincing, powerfully compelling answers that are ultimately useless. We take our life lessons from soft-drink commercials and magazine advertisements. We believe that our lives should have a narrative structure, as lives do in the movies or on TV; indeed many of us act as if we were always on camera—performing instead of living a three-dimensional life. Appearances stand in for real feelings, true connection. It's difficult to distinguish our own thoughts from the thoughts of commentators, pundits, and experts. We are profoundly disconnected from what is real, simple, and true for us. How to turn off and tune into your real voice? That is the work ahead of you.

The work begins with questions. Asking a question can be a sacred act. A real question assumes a dialogue, a link to the source from which answers come. Asking a question is a simple, profound way of initiating a relationship with the energies and powers around and within you. Talking, telling, explaining, complaining, railing, criticizing, praising, lamenting, beseeching—these are the ways we most commonly approach important questions. If we can drop all these for just a moment and simply ask, wonder, become curious about . . . an opening for an answer will be created. Questioning by its very nature is a spiritual practice. We come into dialogue with God, our true nature, wisdom, whatever we choose to call it, whenever we stop, look inside, and take the time and effort to really listen to ourselves.

I learned about the power of asking questions in 1997, when I was thinking about getting married. I was deeply in love with my boyfriend, Duncan. We had been together for four years and were certain about our feelings, but I was still very afraid of getting married. Hadn't all my divorced friends been in love at the time of their marriages? Why would we be any different? In thinking about these things, I realized that getting married wasn't only about being in love and staying in love—it was about creating a life together that we both loved. I couldn't find any resources to help us figure out if we could create such a life together or not, so I began writing down questions about money, friends, home, children, spirituality, and so on. We began answering them together and something really amazing happened: it turned out not to matter whether we agreed, disagreed, or didn't know how to answer any particular question. The act of considering the questions together created a revealing, instructive dialogue between us. As we answered them ("Will we keep our money separately or together?" "Will we share a religion?"), we became more intimate. Our love deepened. After we were married, some answers began to change—some agreements became disagreements, and vice versa; answers emerged for what was previously unanswerable. We kept checking in with each other, using the questions as guides. We learned that it wasn't the answers that were valuable—it was the questioning process. *The Hard Questions for an Authentic Life* uses this process to help you develop this sort of ongoing dialogue with yourself.

Why is tapping into our own inner wisdom so difficult? We long for it, yet we lack the ability to hear ourselves clearly. Our inner wisdom speaks a unique language, made up of a combination of dreams, coincidences, passions, revulsions, and intuitions—and something very powerful that transcends all of those. To understand this voice requires a type of pattern recognition that we're untrained in—but four very important skills can help:

1. Courage
2. Willingness to feel
3. Focus
4. Presence

Courage

Courage is the willingness to open and listen to ourselves, loved ones, enemies, strangers, even circumstance—no matter what is being said. We most often plow through our problems and issues, certain we know the answers already. If only everyone else had the same answer, there would be no problem! Yet, time after time, we use our "answers" to re-create painful situations in relationships, at work, and at home. The Hard Questions ask that we put aside our habitual answers for a little while and approach these questions with a "don't know" mind. If our questions are a genuine inquiry, reliable answers will emerge. Listening requires emptiness and receptivity. A certain kind of space is required, one that is alive, vibrant, ready. Creating this space is a profound act of courage. We are opening ourselves to the truth, no matter what. We are consciously and purposefully stepping beyond our fear.

Willingness to Feel

As we tune in, we may hear things that are exciting, confusing, inspiring, depressing, or unclear. The key is to be willing to notice what is there and feel it. My oddest missteps have occurred as a result of ignoring my own feelings or, worse, not even being able to discern what they are. Feelings are not necessarily the final guide for action, but they are pointing at something we need to know about ourselves—especially our uncomfortable feelings. The unwillingness to tolerate discomfort is often at the root of our worst impulses—we vilify others, subjugate ourselves, overwork, get depressed, isolate, become fearful, overindulge, get angry, or fall into a stupor because we are unable to tolerate discomfort. When we try to avoid or pacify our feelings, we obscure the truth of who we are and what is really happening. The ability to feel and tolerate discomfort is absolutely crucial in searching for an authentic life. We have to be willing to feel anything—no matter what. Can you do this?

Focus

When we do try to tune in, be it through meditation, going for a walk, journaling, or talking with a trusted friend, often the first thing we encounter is other's voices. Parents, colleagues, peers, even characters in movies and songs speak to us about what life should look like. Most of us can't separate these voices from our own. But if we listen carefully and take the time to trace each voice back to its root, we can almost always identify the strands. This requires concentration, an ability to focus, to work with the thoughts, sensations, hopes, and fears that arise, constantly trying to establish their source, unique qualities, direction, and real value. The ability to truly focus brings with it invaluable alertness, sharpness, and precision of mind.

Courage, the willingness to feel, and the ability to focus are not as helpful if we only use them occasionally. They only come to fruition when we are able to practice them over time, even all the time. As we're able to open to ourselves and others, tracking our thoughts, feeling our feelings, and staying focused on how and when they arise, a gap is created between thought and action. This gap gives us an ability to act skillfully, not just from habitual patterns. Invariably, our own inner wisdom, not our beliefs and ideas about inner wisdom, will fill the gap. This space is created through the power of presence, the ability to observe our own minds. So the fourth and most important required skill is awareness, or presence.

Presence

As far as I know, there is only one reliable way to cultivate presence and that is through a regular contemplative practice. There are many to choose from: meditation, journaling, walking, yoga. It doesn't matter which one you choose, so long as you set the intention to take time for contemplation and remain consistent with your chosen practice. Having a daily contemplative practice is like permanently installing a satellite dish outside your house—signals can't reach a dish that is continually moving about, and I don't know why, but our inner voice requires an unmoving target to receive its broadcasts. Spiritual practice creates a steady, reliable way to receive your own wisdom.

If we have the courage to listen, the willingness to feel, the ability to focus, and the skill to remain present no matter what arises, something amazing happens: our own authentic self emerges, moment to moment, in ways that are expected or surprising, convenient or challenging, but more importantly, an accurate reflection of who we really are in that moment. Then our gestures ring true, our relationships, while not necessarily simpler, are genuine, and our professional or creative choices are grounded in our actual gifts.

Asking the Hard Questions can help us do something we aren't really taught to do: make friends with ourselves. Usually, we relate to ourselves with some crazy mixture of egotism and low self-esteem. We are continually judging, berating, haranguing, inflating, defending, and/or consoling ourselves. Rarely do we make the gesture of simple friendship toward ourselves, although we most likely make such gestures throughout the day to others. With our friends, we are interested, caring, and helpful. This process asks you to extend the hand of friendship to yourself.

The Hard Questions offer a place to begin. This book contains one hundred questions about seven essential areas of life: (1) Family, (2) Friendships, (3) Intimate Relationships, (4) Work, (5) Money, (6) Creativity, and (7) Spiritual Life. The questions are part of a process that will help you identify what is working in each area of your life, what isn't working, and why. They will support you as you figure out ways to optimize and honor who you are, and how to work with who and what isn't. Asking the Hard Questions signals that you've made an agreement with yourself to live your authentic life deeply, thoughtfully, and honestly.

How to Answer the Hard Questions

The first step in this process is to really give yourself the chance to carefully and honestly reflect on the questions in each chapter. Don't rush through the process or try to answer all the questions in one sitting. It may take days, weeks, or even months to fully answer these questions. All you will need is the blank pages in this book or your journal, or your computer, depending on where you feel most comfortable recording answers. I encourage you to take the time to write down your answers. Something important occurs when we choose to commit words to paper (or screen); our inner voice crystallizes into formed ideas. This alchemical process creates clarity of thought and allows inner wisdom to come through.

Each time you are ready to approach some of the Hard Questions, find a safe space and some time in which you won't be disturbed, at least thirty minutes or so. Sit in a place that is relaxing and peaceful—your bedroom, at the dining room table, a coffee shop, on a park bench. The important thing is to minimize distractions. If you are at home, turn off phones, pagers, the internet connection. If you have children or roommates, wait until they are asleep or out.

Beyond this, the questions themselves will guide you through the process. Some of them may be a snap to answer; others may seem impossible. They will ask you to consider how you really feel, what you really want, what you truly value. They will help you understand where you feel balanced or unbalanced, nurtured or needy, at ease or awkward. The questions that you are ready to answer will seem juicy and evocative. The ones that aren't for you right now will appear silly or inappropriate. That's okay. Give them another try later.

As you answer the Hard Questions, keep in mind that over time, the answers may change. In fact, I can promise you that the answers *will* change. Finding your authentic life is not like discovering the source of the Amazon and setting up camp there; it's not a place you can identify and mark in time and space. Living your authentic life is a process of getting in tune with your actual thoughts, feelings, needs, and insights, in real time, as they arise, noting as they shift or change. These questions can always be revisited—and each time you do so, they may bring up fresh insights. As you consider ways to answer the questions, work with your responses until you come up with an answer that feels complete, for now. Know that at the moment you set out to seek your inner wisdom, it sets out to seek you too. It may just take some time.

Keep your answers private, or if you feel that you would benefit from discussing them with others, share only with those who can respect the process that goes into answering these questions. It may even be fun to embark on this process with a trusted friend, sharing your answers as you feel ready or willing to. So be patient and let your mind wander over all the possible answers to each question. Pay special attention to the first thoughts that arise, but be willing to set them aside as you consider various answers. Be open and creative with yourself. You will know when one process is complete or impossible to complete at this particular time. You can always go back.

Don't allow yourself to fear-forward into worst case scenarios. Similarly, don't attach yourself to the most hopeful outcome you can imagine. This flies in the face of the New Age ideal: that if you can hold fast to a perfectly sculpted vision of your future, you can pull it toward yourself. Too, this belief suggests an improper placement of the center. So instead of letting your hopes or fears answer the Hard Questions, try to hear your own inner wisdom instead. Let yourself be led to the answers.

As you work with the Hard Questions, I expect you will come to share my realization that living authentically isn't about putting the perfect formula into play (great job + cool apartment + boyfriend =

authentic life) or simply visualizing an outcome and working toward it. It's about being present from moment to moment, starting right now, and then watching as your authentic life emerges. Likely it will surpass your wildest dreams.

I wish you endless courage, a deep willingness to feel, powerful focus, and all the presence of mind you need to create your own unique, resonant, and helpful answers.

CHAPTER 1

Family

It makes complete sense to begin with Hard Questions about family. There is, after all, a good reason why a genealogical chart is commonly referred to as a family tree. We are all rooted in family. For most of us, family history, relationships, and interpersonal dynamics are the soil from which we sprang and the ground upon which we stand. And, generally, our feet are so firmly planted on this ground that we don't give much thought to our root system—until, for whatever reason, it is no longer nourishing us or we feel ourselves becoming rootbound.

By their very nature, therefore, questions about family must also be questions about self. No matter how long we've been on our own or how far we think we've distanced ourselves from the family we grew up with, their rhythms, values, and psychological habits have, whether we realize it or not, left a deep imprint. How many of us have been told, at one time or another, that "you sound just like your mother," or "that's exactly what your father would have said." If you've heard those, or similar comments, were you pleased? Surprised? Did you want to deny it? Whatever your reaction, it probably told you something about your relationship with the family member in question.

Most of us have unresolved issues with our families of origin—issues that we may be attempting to resolve, consciously or not, within the context of our current relationships with them or with others. Family members, for example, are often assigned roles to play within the group—the responsible one, the creative one, the pretty one, to name just a few—and those roles are likely to affect, one way or another, the roles we play with other people in our lives. As a result, the way we relate to parents and siblings as adults can reveal deep truths about all our personal relationships. Bringing those issues into focus in order to examine them more consciously can help us to understand how they may be affecting other areas of our lives—and other relationships—today.

Family bonds—and therefore family issues—are not, however, limited to the family we grew up with. As adults, we expand and develop new branches on our family tree as we marry and have children of our own. And we are also likely to develop all sorts of surrogate "families" of choice among our friends, our colleagues at work, in spiritual or religious groups, and around shared activities such as sports, hobbies, or creative pursuits. Each of these families helps us to create a sense of community and a feeling of belonging, and acts as a source of support and nourishment.

Our relationships with our family of origin and our families of choice can, consciously or unconsciously, affect and reflect upon one another. If we have unrealized or unresolved issues or problems with the former, they can manifest themselves in our relationships with the latter. And what we seek or value in our relationships with one can reveal what we value or feel is lacking in the other. It's important, therefore, as you work with the Hard Questions about family, to consider how your answers relate to all the groups and individuals that feel like family to you.

1. Whom do I consider to be my family? How many families am I a part of? List every person whom you consider to be a part of your family—be it your family of origin, the family you've created through marriage, the family you hope to create, or your families of choice.

_____

_____

_____

_____

_____

_____

_____

_____

2. Take a look at each person on this list and ask yourself the following: How often do we really connect with each other? Is it often enough? Too often? Are we involved enough in each other's life? Too involved? Are there any changes I need to make in terms of time spent with this person or depth of involvement in each other's life?

_____

_____

_____

_____

_____

_____

_____

3. If I have not yet created my own family, would I like to? Is there anyone in my life right now with whom I can imagine creating a family?

_____

_____

_____

_____

_____

_____

_____

_____

4. What would this family look like (just the two of us and our friends, one child, a bunch of kids)? Does this person want to create a family with me? If I don't know, how can I find out?

_____

_____

_____

_____

_____

_____

5. In what ways would I like my family to be similar to the family I grew up in? In what ways would I like it to be different?

_____

_____

_____

_____

_____

_____

_____

6. What values did I gain from my family of origin? The three most helpful? The three least helpful? Where do I notice these values showing up in my current life, with my current family (if applicable), and with my friends and intimate partners?

_____

_____

_____

_____

_____

_____

_____

7. How have these values evolved or changed as I've become an independent adult? Has this created conflict within myself or within my family? If so, is there anything I can do or say to resolve these conflicts? What is the very next step I can take in this process?

_____

_____

_____

_____

_____

_____

_____

_____

_____

8. What conflicts exist within my immediate family (whether of origin or of marriage)? Is there any way to resolve them? Is there anyone I need to forgive? If so, for what? Whether or not the conflict involves me directly, what can I do to create healing within the family? Is there a conversation I need to have, a letter I can write, or an internal shift I can make to start the healing process?

_____

_____

_____

_____

_____

_____

_____

9. If I'm married or in a committed relationship, does my spouse or intimate partner feel like "family" to me? If so, what is it about our relationship that makes it feel like family? If not, why not? Are there things I can do to deepen our sense of family?

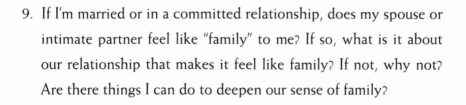

_____

_____

_____

_____

_____

_____

_____

_____

10. What do I really need that my family is unable to give me? Are there unresolved issues of psychological or physical security? Emotional connection and support? Is there some other way to get these needs met? Is there a conversation I need to have with a family member, clergy, or therapist to help me with my unmet needs?

_____

_____

_____

_____

_____

_____

_____

11. What do I wish my family understood about me? Knew about me? Liked about me? Are there contributions I make that I feel go unappreciated? Are there things I like about myself that my family doesn't seem to recognize and value? Does my family "see" and appreciate who I really am? If not, how can I bring them more fully into my inner life? Or become reconciled to the idea that this may never happen?

_____

_____

_____

_____

_____

_____

_____

12. What am I expected to contribute to my family? Am I the sole breadwinner? A key contributor to family income? Who is the central emotional caregiver? Who is responsible for household chores such as cooking, cleaning, repairs, bookkeeping? Am I comfortable with the roles I play? If not, what can I do to make the sorts of changes I'd like?

_____

_____

_____

_____

_____

_____

_____

_____

13. What holidays or events do I share with my family? Which would I like to share? Do we celebrate each other, important events, and happy times? Do we have a way of supporting each other during difficult times?

_____

_____

_____

_____

_____

_____

_____

14. If I don't feel that I'm part of any family, what can I do to create family in my life? Are there professional, spiritual, leisure, or creative groups I can reach out to or join?

_____

_____

◆ CHAPTER 2 ◆

Friendships

We all think we know what the word "friendship" means. We all can name a number of people we call friends. And I'm sure we all can remember the feeling of joy we had as children when someone told us he or she wanted to be our friend. Or we remember the sadness and confusion we experienced when someone said he or she *didn't* want to be our friend, or didn't want to be our friend anymore.

What many of us haven't fully considered, however, is the degree to which a friend can be either supportive or destructive of our ability to lead an authentic life. Most of our relationships—either familiar or collegial—are not created by choice, and therefore we *must* find a way to make them work. It is in our friendships that we are able to exercise the most choice. Too many of us, however, seem to maintain relationships with friends just because we've known them so long or because we've fallen into the habit of thinking of them as friends.

Both the pleasures and the pain of friendship began for most of us when we were children, and haven't diminished in adulthood. I remember as a teenager spending all day with my best friend and then rushing home to call her. We talked on the phone for hours, laughing or complaining. The connection between us was incredibly precious to me. For most of us, the need for just such close friendships has not diminished as we've matured, but the opportunity and means for creating such relationships have. As adults, making and keeping friends seems to require more work and attention. The Hard Questions can help create that focus.

But also as children, adolescents, and teenagers some of us may have yearned so much to belong to a particular group or to count a particular person among our friends that we were willing to compromise our values. And as adults we may do the same thing in more subtle ways—keeping our mouths shut when we disagree with what's being said or participating in a questionable activity simply to be included. When we do that, however, we're not being true to ourselves, and our "friends" are not really our friends because they don't really know who we are. The Hard Questions can help you to identify those times when you may have hidden your true self in the name of a questionable friendship.

Friendship can be a valuable tool—perhaps even the *most* valuable tool we have to help us lead an authentic life. Friends can look out for our interests, support us not only in the best times but also in the worst. They can provide comfort and companionship. And, perhaps most important of all, they can keep us honest by being truthful when we ask for their opinion or advice. But friends can also distract us from our goals and resent our efforts to change.

The Hard Questions about friendship can help you to focus on what it really means to be a friend, a "good" friend in every sense of the word. They can also help you to identify those people in your life whom you've been counting among your friends but who may not have your best interests at heart and may, therefore, be standing in the way of your being true to yourself and leading a life that is authentic to your needs, values, and goals. And finally, they can help you to determine whether you are being as good a friend for others as you want them to be for you.

15. What does the word friendship mean to me? What purpose do I think friends serve in my life? What qualities do I expect to find in the people I number among my friends?

_____

_____

_____

_____

_____

_____

16. Who are the five people I would count as my closest friends? Do they serve the purpose and exhibit the qualities I identified as defining the word "friendship"?

17. Are there any people I count among my friends whose qualities are antithetical to those I believe a friend should have? If so, why is it that I've maintained my friendship with them? Are they providing me with something—emotionally, psychologically, or practically—that makes me reluctant to end the relationship? If so, is what I'm getting really "worth it" to me? Am I too afraid to confront the person or situation? If the latter, what might give me the courage I need?

18. Who are my oldest friends? Why is it that we've remained
    friends for so long? Would I seek them as my friends if I were
    meeting them today rather than at the stage in my life when we
    met originally?

19. Who are my newest friends? How did we meet? What are the
    qualities in these people that caused me to seek and maintain
    their friendship?

_____

_____

_____

_____

_____

_____

20. Do I want to broaden my group of friends or am I happy with just those I have now? (Some people need a lot of friends, possibly to satisfy a variety of needs, while others are happy with just a few close, friendly relationships. Which group do I fall into?) If I want more friends, why is that? Am I in some way dissatisfied with those I have? Am I seeking something from my friends that they are unable to give?

_____

_____

_____

_____

_____

_____

_____

21. Am I as an individual involved in some pursuit or challenge, the enjoyment or outcome of which might be enhanced by my having the advice, companionship, or help of a new friend?

_____

_____

_____

_____

22. If I am somehow dissatisfied with or disappointed by one or more of my friendships, why do I feel that way? Am I seeking something that this friend is unable or unwilling to provide? Have we outgrown one another? Have my feelings for this person changed? Have my friend's feelings about me changed? How might I develop a deeper understanding of the dynamics between us?

_____

_____

_____

_____

_____

_____

_____

_____

_____

23. If I want to make new friends, how can I go about that? Is there anyone at work with whom I'd like to develop a deeper connection? Is there a club or organization I could join or an activity I could pursue that would put me in contact with people whose interests and values are similar to my own?

_____

_____

_____

_____

_____

_____

_____

24. Do I find it difficult to make new friends? Is my manner open and welcoming or do I appear standoffish and aloof? Am I shy? Do I find it difficult to talk to new people? Is there something I can do consciously to let people know I would be happy to develop a friendship with them?

_____

_____

_____

_____

25. If I were to ask my good friends, what would they tell me are the qualities they value in me? What would they say it is that makes me as good a friend to them as they are to me? Do I live up to my own definition of what a good friend should be? Do I have qualities that I think my friends undervalue? If so, what are they? Are there aspects of my personality that I would like to "work on" so that I could be a better friend? If so, what are they?

26. When I look around me, do I see friendships between other people that I think are more mutually supportive, nourishing, and rewarding than my own? Can I identify particular qualities in these people that make their friendships so successful? Are these qualities I could nurture in myself and/or seek in others?

_____

_____

_____

_____

_____

_____

_____

_____

27. If I've identified people I number among my friends who consistently ask me to act in ways that are antithetical to my authentic self, or who don't value me for the person I am, what can I do to minimize the emotional and psychological toll they are taking on my life? Or would it be to my benefit to cut myself off completely from these people? If so, what can I do to accomplish this in the kindest way possible? If not, why is it I believe I should continue the relationship at least on some level?

_____

_____

_____

_____

_____

_____

_____

_____

28. If I spent more time nurturing those friends who are supportive and who enhance my life, if I spent more time nurturing the qualities that make me a good friend, if I devoted less time to those people who are draining my energy and making my life more difficult, would I have taken a significant step toward leading a more authentic life? If my answer to these questions is yes, then what are the steps I can take to start down that road immediately?

_____

_____

_____

_____

_____

_____

_____

◆ CHAPTER 3 ◆
Intimate Relationships

Most people want to be involved in a lasting intimate relation-ship. We spend a lot of time and energy searching for some-one to love and, inevitably, making plenty of missteps along the way. When I was younger—and I don't think I'm unusual in this re-gard—I used to imagine my beloved: his looks, interests, talents, how he would love me. Some of my ideas were based on my deep-est needs and desires, some were borrowed from songs, movies, or books, but somehow, from this eclectic collection of sources, I came up with a definition of the person I could love and why. When I did fall in love with the man who became my husband, however, I fell in love with a man who had very little in common with the guy I'd imagined. In fact, the guy I'd imagined became an impediment at some point, and I had to dispose of him in order to be in this au-thentically loving relationship. That realization was a powerful les-son in intimacy and authenticity: no matter how well we think we know ourselves, or how clear we are about what we're looking for in a partner, we will most likely be surprised again and again by the pleasure and panic induced by love.

Our ideas, fantasies, and projections about what life *should* look like are, in fact, among the biggest obstacles to living and loving authentically. We think life should match our ideas about what life should be, and our most powerful illusions are often reserved for those we love most deeply. Thus, the more we love, the more we commit; the more we invest in another, the more we expect that person to conform to our fantasy of what a partner should look like and how he or she should feel and behave.

It takes a lot of effort not to confuse our partner with our fantasies of who our partner should be, but letting go of those expectations is, in fact, the first step to authentic intimacy. I hope the Hard Questions will help you begin to identify your fantasies about love and your partner and see how they compare to the realities. This— releasing your partner from your projections about whom he or she should be in order to embrace whom he or she is—is actually a profound spiritual act, one that requires as much courage, willingness to feel, focus, and presence as you've got!

Our biggest ally in this task is the simple act of falling in love. In my opinion, falling in love is as close as most of us will ever get to feeling the grace of God. I believe that no experience is as transformational or joyous, or as likely to show us that we are so much more than we ever thought, that our lives can be richer and deeper and more lovely than we ever dreamed. It is not, however, *all* there is. It is actually just the first step.

To fall in love is, without doubt, a life-transforming experience. When we fall in love, we become immersed in a powerful contemplation of our beloved. Our every thought, breath, vision, and dream is about him or her. But the act of "falling" is, by its very nature, impermanent, and at some point, when our contemplative retreat comes to an end, we must figure out a way to bring our relationship into the world of working, eating, leisure, and our other relationships—family, friends, colleagues, and so on. Although we may be very happy out on dates with our beloved, it may be a different matter altogether to decide which holidays to celebrate, figure out whether or not to pool bank accounts, or discuss the possibility of children.

These two poles—falling in love and creating a life together that you both love—are very different entities. Most of us believe that the former will naturally lead to the latter. Unfortunately, however, the two have nothing in common. Most of us lean toward one pole or the other: You may seek the pleasure of falling in love over and over again, believing that once the "falling" is over, it means the love is gone. Or you may think of the "falling" part as a means of getting to the life you want: the home, family, community that you seek. It's important, however, to give equal attention to both, to not grip either phase too tightly, because neither one is any good without the other. The Hard Questions about intimate relationships can help you identify what you seek from love, how satisfied or dissatisfied you are with your current situation (regardless of whether or not you're in a relationship), what your gifts are as a lover, and your deficits.

Many of us seem to re-create the same relationship over and over with different partners. If you see that pattern in your own life, the Hard Questions can help you identify your unhealthy patterns and determine how they may be playing out in your relationships.

The Hard Questions about intimate relationships use the words "he" and "him" when talking about your partner. This is for simplicity's sake. Please feel free to substitute the other pronoun. Too, an attempt was made to word the questions in a way that would work for those in a relationship or those seeking a relationship. If questions about "current relationships" don't apply to you, feel free to think back to your last significant relationship and apply the question to it.

29. When I consider my priorities, where do I place my need for an intimate relationship? Is it the most important thing—or among the most important things—in my life?

_____

_____

_____

_____

_____

_____

_____

30. Am I currently satisfied with the degree of intimacy I'm experiencing? Whether or not I'm in a settled relationship, am I experiencing emotional, sexual, or spiritual intimacy with anyone?

_____

_____

_____

_____

_____

_____

_____

31. What do I most want to share with my intimate partner? Emotional support? Sexuality? Friendship? Spiritual connection? Intellectual rapport? A shared lifestyle and values? Fun? Something else? How do I prioritize these? How does my partner prioritize them?

_____

_____

_____

_____

_____

_____

_____

32. When I'm in an intimate relationship, how do my priorities shift? Does my relationship take precedence over all other aspects of my life? Do relationship priorities take precedence over other priorities or vice versa? Does this balance work for me? How does my partner order his priorities? Does this balance work for me?

_____

_____

_____

_____

_____

_____

_____

_____

33. Does my current relationship satisfy the needs I have identified? If so, does my partner know how much I cherish these aspects of our relationship?

_____

_____

_____

_____

_____

_____

34. In what ways does my current relationship *not* satisfy these needs? Is my partner aware of the fact that these needs are not being met? Have I communicated these feelings to him? If not, how can I do that? If we are communicating, is there any way to make our communication more effective?

_____

_____

_____

_____

_____

_____

_____

_____

35. What special gifts do I have to offer as a lover or partner? Am I steadfast, giving, exciting, patient, sensitive, loyal, protective, fun? What other qualities can I identify as special in me?

_____

_____

_____

_____

_____

_____

36. What qualities prevent me from being a better partner? Am I jealous, clingy, selfish, too demanding, unreliable, flaky, fearful? What other negative qualities can I identify in myself? Am I willing to change? How capable am I (and is my partner) of recognizing and working with these issues in a healthy way?

_____

_____

_____

_____

_____

_____

_____

_____

37. What qualities does my partner most appreciate in me? What does he love most about me? Are they the same gifts I've identified in myself? What does he criticize me for? Are they the same flaws I've recognized in myself? Is he loving me for who I really am? Are we clear with each other about these likes and dislikes? In a healthy way? An unhealthy way (by yelling and criticizing rather than discussing and exploring)? How honest are we really able to be with each other?

_____

_____

_____

_____

_____

_____

_____

_____

38. What qualities do I most appreciate in my partner? What qualities do I dislike? Have I discussed these with him in a healthy and productive way? Do I see him as he sees himself? Do I value him for the things he values in himself?

_____

_____

_____

_____

_____

_____

_____

39. Is there something missing for me in our relationship—a spiritual component, personal space, shared interests, a commitment, children, simple fun? Have I discussed these things with my partner? What is missing for my partner? Am I open to discussing these things with him? Do we have any sense of how to resolve unmet needs?

_____

_____

_____

_____

_____

_____

_____

_____

40. What has been left unsaid in our relationship? What can I *not* ask him for? Is there some emotional, spiritual, physical, or practical aspect of our relationship that I would like to explore but am too afraid to ask about? What circumstances would make me feel safe enough to ask for what I want or need?

_____

_____

_____

_____

_____

_____

_____

41. Are there problems that seem to crop up for me in one relationship after another? Have I been able to identify them for myself? Am I experiencing any of these problems in my current relationship? Have I discussed them with my partner? Are we trying to work on them together?

_____

_____

_____

_____

_____

_____

_____

_____

42. Is there something I can learn from these recurrent problems? From the way my relationships typically end? Am I usually the person who leaves or the one who is left? How do I handle the breakups?

_____

_____

_____

_____

_____

_____

_____

_____

43. Is there a past relationship that still haunts me? That I still feel connected to or affected by? What can I identify about that relationship that made it so meaningful? Is there anything I can learn from this that would allow me to lay it to rest and perhaps make my current relationship more satisfying or help me to find more meaningful relationships in the future?

_____

_____

_____

_____

_____

_____

_____

_____

44. What kind of relationship do I hope to be in (with my current or another partner) in a year? Five years? Twenty-five years? What can I learn from the Hard Questions that will help me to achieve that goal?

_____

_____

_____

◆ CHAPTER 4 ◆

Work

If you are truly happy in your work, if it fulfills your dreams and aspirations for yourself, and if, in addition, you are being well compensated for what you do—earning enough to support your leisure activities and preferred lifestyle—you are truly one of the lucky ones. But if this isn't the case, it doesn't mean you can't achieve these things or never will. In fact, the Hard Questions in this chapter are designed to help you find a way to join that happy pantheon.

For most of us, work and money are inextricably connected. We spend our working lives trying to make enough money to live comfortably. And very often, even if we're lucky enough to meet that need, immediately a new, equally important need arises: the need to maintain our position. We become "addicted" to our salary, our title, the standing our position confers on us in the eyes of our family and community. I'm sure we've all stayed with jobs we knew were wrong for us, jobs that actually made us unhappy, just because we didn't want to give up the money or image the position provided.

For many years, I worked in the music business as an executive at various record labels. My last job in the business should have been my "dream job." I was hired to create a brand-new division for an existing record company. My mandate was to produce CDs for people interested in spirituality and wellness. That was perfect for me—a way to blend my spiritual life with my professional capabilities. The company was well funded, and I was offered a salary significantly higher than what I'd been earning. Perfect, yes? No!

I remember one day returning to my office from a meeting with one of the best-selling spirituality authors in the world. We had been discussing a project of combining a book with music. I rushed up the stairs in order not to be late for an appointment with my boss. We were to discuss all the financial and legal details of what could be a very important deal for our new company. Unfortunately, he wasn't there and had left no word. Later I found out that he had already made the deal without discussing it with me and had gone out to lunch. I would have to manage the business brought in by this new deal even though I'd had no input in its creation. I felt stung and deflated. As I walked back to my office, I couldn't help being struck by the difference between the image we wished to create for our company—supportive, compassionate, and meaningful—and the way we treated one another.

At work, it's not at all unusual to face insults, intrigues, power plays, interpersonal conflicts, and insecurities about position and value. When we experience these issues in our relationships with family, friends, or lovers, there are many books, support groups, and therapists we can turn to for help. We're encouraged to face such difficulties consciously by exploring our feelings, communicating our needs, and expecting to be treated with respect and honesty. When the same issues arise at work, however, we're often out of luck when it comes to finding a healthy, mutually supportive way to deal with them that doesn't threaten our job security. We tolerate behaviors at work that we would never tolerate in other relationships, perhaps because work is so intimately tied up with survival and self-image. Our sense that without steady work or regular income our lives will become immediately destabilized (whether or not this is true) cannot only keep us in a job that is stressful and unfulfilling, it can also prevent us from being honest with ourselves about how we feel about our profession, colleagues, even about our own aspirations. What I've noticed—about myself as well as my friends—is that we're more willing to compromise our values, priorities, and needs at work than anywhere else in our lives. The Hard Questions can help you take an honest look at just where your current work situation does or does not mesh with your values, priorities, and aspirations. And if the "fit" isn't right for you, these same questions can help you begin to find a way to shift gears or get the ones driving your career to make things run more smoothly.

Obviously, we have to be practical, and I don't want to suggest pulling the plug on a job without having a realistic plan in place, but whether we decide to stick with or leave an unhappy position, we can all benefit from knowing the truth of our feelings and needs. The Hard Questions can help you assess the reasons you might want to stick with or switch jobs.

Beyond money and position, however, there is the even more basic question of whether or not you've even given serious thought to what kind of work you really *want* to do. You may simply have "fallen into" your work right after school or because an opportunity presented itself, without ever giving your goals and aspirations much serious consideration. Or you may be aware that your work is not really fulfilling and yet have no idea what it is you really *want* to do. I know that throughout my own life—and I'm far from alone in this—I've felt an unnamable longing, a powerful wish to devote myself to work that felt predestined, that took advantage of and helped me evolve my unique gifts and wish to contribute to the benefit of others. I just didn't know what that work would be. "Tell me what I should do with my life," I've often prayed, "and I will give everything to it." The Hard Questions about work can help you begin to assess your real gifts and aspirations.

Before you begin answering the questions, I'd like to ask you to please take a quiet moment and really allow yourself to *feel* your aspirations. We often don't permit ourselves to feel the fullness of our desires, the richness of our gifts—it can be too scary or embarrassing. Let yourself actually feel what they are. Do you know what they are, precisely? Or do you simply have a general sense? Are they simple, sensible, nonsensical, impossible, doable? Observe the images, sensations, and thoughts that come to mind. Whatever they are, make note of them, bring them out into the open, and let them begin to breathe. Hold them in your mind as you answer the following questions.

45. Am I able to elucidate my professional values, goals, and aspirations? If so, what are they? Even if I can't be specific in my description, what do I know about myself in this regard?

_____

_____

_____

_____

_____

_____

_____

_____

46. Which, if any, of the aspirations I've identified am I not allowing myself to manifest? Do I have gifts or goals that I'm too afraid to pursue? Do I have a skill that I'm not using at work? What is it? Do I use it elsewhere in my life?

_____

_____

_____

_____

_____

_____

_____

47. How much (or little) does my current job reflect my values, goals, and aspirations? Is there a connection between my work and these ideals? If I want more of a connection, is there any way I can cause my current work situation to more fully reflect my values? How? When?

_____

_____

_____

_____

_____

_____

_____

48. If I am happy in my current career path but do not feel I'm advancing, growing, or learning as quickly as I'd like, is there anything I can do to change that?

_____

_____

_____

_____

49. How do my coworkers see me? How do I want them to see me? How does my boss see me? How do I want him or her to see me? Treat me? Offer me? What steps can I take to effect the changes I'd like to see?

_____

_____

_____

_____

_____

_____

_____

_____

50. If there is no chance (or wish) to bring my current work situation into alignment with my values, goals, and aspirations, what new situation would be more likely to create this alignment? Do I know of any such position? Do I know anyone who does the work I think I would like to do? Would I benefit from a conversation with them?

---

51. Regardless of "feasibility," what is my true passion for my work life? (Don't be afraid to name it.) Can I describe it? In detail? In generalities? Is there anything I do in my life currently, whether I get paid for it or not, that reflects this passion? Is there anything I *could* be doing?

_____

_____

_____

_____

_____

52. If money were no object and failure was not possible, what would my professional aspiration(s) be?

_____

_____

_____

53. What are my best skills in the workplace? Is there a field more closely related to my personal goals and aspirations in which I could use the skills I have to earn a living?

_____

_____

_____

_____

_____

_____

54. What skills do I lack? Is there any way I can begin to acquire the skills that would allow me to fulfill these aspirations?

_____

_____

_____

_____

_____

_____

_____

55. Do I have anyone to model myself after professionally? Who? Whose career do I aspire to emulate? Why? Do I have a relationship with this person? Would I benefit from a conversation with him or her?

_____

_____

_____

_____

_____

_____

_____

56. Which colleagues, friends, or family members really support me in my professional aspirations? Who can I rely on for inspiration, backing, motivation?

_____

_____

_____

_____

_____

_____

_____

57. What role does work currently play in my life? Is my life built around my work or is my work built around my life? How happy am I with this balance? If I'm not happy, is there anything I can do that would help me begin to change that balance?

_____

_____

_____

_____

_____

58. What practical steps can I take right now to get the support I
    need to transform my work life into something more fulfilling
    and authentic to my values and goals?

_____

_____

_____

_____

✦ CHAPTER 5 ✦

Money

If you were ever in any doubt about the high level of importance money plays in most people's lives, a quick trip to the bookstore would quickly dispel those doubts. The shelves are filled with books telling us how to make more money, how to live better on less, how to budget, how to plan for our financial future, how to resolve money issues between spouses or partners, and how men's approach to money issues differs from women's. The variations on these themes seem to be endless.

Of all the subjects addressed in this book, money may be the most difficult of all to deal with honestly and openly. (I know it is for me.) Most of us feel enormous discomfort when we think about money—how much we have, earn, owe, want to have, fear not having. It's also a very difficult subject to talk about with others. I know much more about my friends' sex lives than I do about their financial situations. And money issues are very often the ones that cause the most problems in intimate relationships. Somehow, the qualities of openness, vulnerability, and honesty with which we discuss other important topics with loved ones seem to go missing when the subject of money arises. Friends who have no fear of talking about their most intimate hopes and dreams clam up when it comes to issues of income and debt. My beloved husband and I are able to discuss the most carefully observed and subtle aspects of our positive and negative feelings for each other, but we invariably end up yelling (him) or crying (me) when it comes to talking about our finances. Why?

One of the reasons, I think, is that we've all been sent very contradictory messages about money. On the one hand, we've been taught that we *must* think about it if we are to be fiscally responsible adults, and, on the other hand, we've been told that it isn't polite or good form to discuss the very subject we've been told is so important in all our lives. How do we honor both those teachings without making ourselves just a little bit crazy? How do we resolve any money problems we might have if we're not supposed to discuss them? Because we're so reluctant to talk about money issues, many of us engage in a kind of fantastical thinking that may or may not have anything to do with what's really happening in our lives.

We tend to imagine that having more money would solve virtually all the problems in our lives. Most of us don't think we have enough—or that we'll ever have enough. And that means we can never stop thinking about it.

At various times in my life, I've thought the following about my present and future finances:

I have to give up my creative and professional dreams and focus on making money.

I have to give up a steady income in order to realize my creative and professional dreams.

If I do a really good job, I'll make enough money.

I don't know how, but I assume that eventually I'll make enough money.

I don't know why, but I'm pretty sure I'll never make enough money.

When/if I get married, my money problems will be solved.

Other people seem to have a knack for making money, but I don't.

Once I figure out what I'm "supposed" to be doing with my life, money issues will just automatically take care of themselves.

I'll never have enough money to support myself in my "golden years."

I'm sure something or someone will come along to solve my financial problems, so I'm just not going to worry about them now.

I'm sure you've had similar "flashes of insight," and I'm equally sure they've been just as unhelpful for you as they have been for me. Each one of these thoughts was simply an indication of my most recent state of confusion about money at that time in my life. I continually erred (and continue to err) in figuring out how to take care of myself financially, asking for enough money when assessing work opportunities, sharing financial information with my husband, figuring out how to save, spend, and invest. Why is this subject so frightening?

Money can mean security, love, power, freedom, or all of the above. How you view it, the qualities with which you imbue it, will depend on the circumstances in which you grew up, lessons learned from early earning experiences, the image you seek to portray to others, and, finally, your actual aspirations. Some of us seem to worry about it all the time, whether we need to or not, while others take the ostrich approach and assume that if they just don't think about it or worry about it, the problem (if there is one) will magically resolve itself.

It's because different people's styles of dealing with money are so different from one another that the subject can be so difficult and divisive in relationships. One partner might believe in balancing the checkbook to the penny while the other never balances it at all. One might believe that if we take care of ourselves today, tomorrow will take care of itself, while the other insists on saving as much as possible for the future. One person might value the comforts and possessions money can buy while the other would gladly give them up for a simpler, less harried, but also less lucrative lifestyle. One might be a risk taker when it comes to investing while the other has a deathly fear of losing even a portion of what he or she has attained.

The Hard Questions can help you figure out what you value money for, the power you hope it will bring you (or fear it will deny you), as well as the role it plays in your intimate relationships.

59. How urgent an issue is money in my life, right now? Am I satisfied with what I have or am making? Dissatisfied? Do I spend too much time in pursuit of money? Not enough time?

_____

_____

_____

_____

_____

_____

_____

_____

60. What purpose does money serve in my life? Do I value it for
the security it brings, the options it gives me, the pleasure it
provides?

_____

_____

_____

_____

_____

_____

61. What are my most urgent money worries? Do I worry that I
will never have, make, or save enough? Are my worries valid?
How can I work with my fears?

_____

_____

_____

_____

_____

_____

_____

_____

62. How much importance do I give to money when making career decisions? Is this appropriate? Would I benefit from giving money more importance in these decisions? Less?

_____

_____

_____

_____

_____

_____

_____

63. Does the money I earn make me feel valued for the work I do? If not, what salary or remuneration *would* make me feel valued? Am I prepared to work toward this goal? With whom do I need to have this discussion? What do I need in terms of support or information to begin?

_____

_____

_____

_____

_____

_____

_____

_____

64. Am I financially responsible? How good (or bad) am I at managing my finances? Do I have an adequate system for keeping financial records? Do I spend within my means or am I constantly overspending? Do I hold on to money too tightly? Am I so afraid of overspending that I deny myself or my family? If I overspend or am in fear of overspending, is there some way I could set up my finances so that I felt more comfortable?

_____

_____

_____

_____

_____

_____

65. How much money do I have right now? How much debt? How comfortable or uncomfortable am I with the amount I have and the amount I owe? How can I increase my comfort levels? Am I on a budget? Do I need one? Do I have a plan for paying down debt as quickly as possible? Do I need one? Who or what can help me become clear and responsible about saving money and paying off debt?

_____

_____

_____

_____

_____

_____

_____

66. How much money do I want to be making in a year? Five years? Ten years? Twenty-five years? Do I have (or need) a plan for reaching these goals? How can I make such a plan?

_____

_____

_____

_____

_____

_____

_____

67. Do I currently support myself financially? Am I comfortable
with this situation? If so, do I expect to be doing so for the rest
of my life? What circumstances might change this? Am I supporting anyone else financially? Am I okay with this? If so, do I
expect to be doing so for the rest of my life? What circumstances might change this?

_____

_____

_____

_____

_____

_____

_____

68. What did I learn about money from my family of origin? Which lessons were valuable? Which were detrimental? How do these lessons show up in my life today? Am I comfortable with this? If not, what steps could I take to honor the valuable lessons or diminish the effect of the detrimental ones?

_____

_____

_____

_____

_____

_____

_____

69. If I'm in a committed relationship, does my partner's approach to money management mesh with my own? Do we agree on how money should be spent, saved, and/or invested?

_____

_____

_____

_____

_____

_____

70. How comfortable am I with the way my partner manages and makes money? Are we able to discuss finances openly and honestly? If not, why? How can we improve our ability to communicate? Are there any pressing issues that require a conversation right now? Do I feel comfortable initiating the conversation? If not, what can I do to make having this conversation more comfortable for me?

_____

_____

_____

_____

_____

_____

_____

71. Are money issues creating tension in our relationship? If so, is there anything my partner and I can do to help us resolve these issues? Would we benefit from seeing a financial consultant?

_____

_____

_____

_____

_____

_____

_____

_____

72. If I knew I had all the money I would ever need, would my life change substantially? In what way? What would I do that's different from the way I live now?

_____

_____

_____

_____

_____

_____

_____

_____

◆ CHAPTER 6 ◆

Creativity

M ost of us think of creativity as a special kind of skill, talent, or gift bestowed upon painters, musicians, writers—in other words, artists, people who are in some way "gifted," "unusual," or "unconventional." We also think of creativity as the opposite of practicality, which we associate with responsibility or "real life." Most of us have been taught that as we mature we need to become more practical and responsible, and we must, therefore, give up our creativity—however we express it—because it is a luxury we can no longer afford. However, these are both misconceptions. Creativity is present in everyone, all the time—in the way we see, smell, taste, touch, and hear the world around us. To be creative is simply to be present in the moment, to feel what is happening around and within us right now. Our creativity is what gives meaning to every moment of our lives.

In every moment we have two choices. One choice is to rely on habitual patterns of response to the events of our lives. "I have to pay a visit to my mother—she always makes me feel bad about myself," is an example of a habitual response to a particular situation. The other choice is to step outside of our habits and see what is really, truly happening, right now, within us and around us. It may be the same thing that has happened before or it may be completely new and different. The creative part is allowing oneself to sense and experience each moment with complete freshness and openness, *as if* it were happening for the first time. Because, in fact, it is.

If you are a mother or father, I'm sure you've experienced this many times—your child comes home from school and, on some days, before the door shuts behind him, you know his mood, how his day went, what he needs from you right now. This is a supremely creative act. All your senses immediately "click in" to the energies at hand and you just know what is really going on. When you're in touch with your creativity, everything becomes clearer: You know how to respond to those around you. You know what you need in a given situation. You are completely present.

The ability to be present actually gives you the skill to act authentically. Without this presence, your actions, reactions, thoughts, and feelings stem from *ideas* about reality rather than reality itself. And so, in this sense, being creative and being authentic are indivisible; they are one and the same. Both share the quality of being in the moment, without preconceived thoughts, concepts, or ideas. In fact, creativity (as defined here) may be the single greatest tool there is for living life authentically. The good news is that it's a tool we all possess!

It's possible to bring a creative sense to everything we do, and I would bet any amount of money that you already bring enormous amounts of it to some area of your life. You just don't think of it as being creative. Perhaps you always seem to know just what to say to children when they're crying. Or possibly you have an innate sense of style and chic. Maybe you're known as a really great cook. Cooking, in fact, provides the perfect metaphor for what it means to be creative. You can follow a recipe and cook a dish exactly as described without ever tasting or smelling it, and the dish will be as good as the recipe, but cooking it doesn't require a great deal of creativity. Or you could look at the recipe and decide to use a bit more spice, or add another ingredient, or substitute one kind of vegetable for another. As you prepare the dish, you taste, sniff, stir, and adjust the seasoning or add more liquid, or stir. You are completely present and aware as you cook that dish and it is a product of your creativity.

It's certain that you possess natural creativity in one area or another, and it's just as certain that, somewhere along the line, you didn't receive quite enough nurturance for your gifts. Julia Cameron, author of the best creativity tool I've ever encountered, *The Artist's Way*, describes our culture as "anti-art." We don't recognize, appreciate, or support art in our culture except perhaps as items of status, taste, or cool. The pure, raw impulse to create is undervalued. We simply don't know *how* to nurture or appreciate creativity in ourselves and others—it seems too scary or irrelevant. One way is to just start where you are, with those areas or activities that call to you naturally. It doesn't matter whether you're drawn to performance art or knitting, writing books or reading them, drawing flowers or planting them; I feel sure that there is something you already do that involves your imagination and intuition.

Where have you noticed your unique talents? Where have you received encouragement? Discouragement? The Hard Questions can help you identify friends and foes of your creativity. These questions aren't meant to help you discover that you're really meant to be a poet or a pianist (although that would be great!), but rather to help you identify who and what help you to feel connected to your senses and your own inner knowing.

Finally, the Hard Questions ask you to focus on pleasure. The ability to feel and experience pleasure is in itself a creative act. Think about what truly brings you delight. One of the primary characteristics of real pleasure is the quality of surprise. We are taken by pleasure; we can't take it. We never know when it will occur. Much as we try, we can't actually author or possess pleasure; we can only be open to it and embrace it when it arises. In fact, the more we try to possess it, the less pleasurable the result will feel. Pleasure, like creativity, simply materializes. And because creativity and pleasure are so related—both requiring presence, openness, and receptivity—they can also enhance one another. Deep pleasure, even joy, results from rousing your own creativity. Likewise, invoking pleasure (what is pleasurable for *you*) enhances and feeds your natural creative impulses. It's a mistake to think that art, of whatever sort, results only from suffering. In truth, it's as—or more—likely to flow from pleasure. So the Hard Questions about creativity also ask you to consider what does and does not give you pleasure.

73. Do I think of myself as a creative person? Everyone has special gifts of intelligence, compassion, insight, ingenuity, style, etc: What are mine?

_____

_____

_____

_____

_____

_____

_____

_____

74. Are there any people in my life whom I consider to be particularly creative? In what ways does their creativity manifest itself? Can seeing how they approach life help me to awaken my own creative gifts, even if they are very different?

_____

_____

_____

_____

_____

_____

_____

75. Do I possess any particular creative gifts that I'm too shy or embarrassed to admit, maybe even to myself? Am I able to "own" my gifts; do I feel comfortable admitting them, even to myself? If I were to allow these gifts to manifest in my life, how would my life change?

_____

_____

_____

_____

_____

_____

_____

_____

76. How and where do I express my creative gifts? In writing, painting, cooking, childcare, the way I dress, gardening, conversation, praying? Any or all of these can be outlets for creativity. What are mine? Are they adequate for my self-expression? If not, what changes can I make to provide myself with greater opportunities for creative expression?

_____

_____

_____

_____

_____

_____

_____

77. With whom do I feel most comfortable being my most powerful, gifted self? What do these people do to make me feel this way? With whom do I feel the least comfortable? What do these people do to make me feel this way?

_____

_____

_____

_____

_____

_____

_____

_____

78. What situation or situations do I continually and habitually respond to in ways that cause my own or others' unhappiness? How might I employ my creativity to respond differently the next time I encounter this situation? What would my new, more creative response look and feel like to me? To others?

_____

_____

_____

_____

_____

_____

79. Are there people or groups whose support would nourish and help me to enhance my creativity? If so, how do I locate them and verify my assumption that their support would indeed be nourishing?

_____

_____

_____

_____

_____

_____

_____

_____

80. What places or circumstances seem to connect me with my creativity? Museums, books, nature, meditation, and intimate relationships are a few examples of places, activities, or situations that might evoke creativity. Do I spend enough time and energy exploring these areas? When I do find myself in one of these situations, am I able to slow down and really notice what goes on for me, or do I speed right through it?

_____

_____

_____

_____

_____

_____

_____

81. What tools support my creativity: journaling, meditation, walking, taking classes, doing creative projects with friends, taking time for contemplation, others? Do I allow enough time in my life for these pursuits?

_____

_____

_____

_____

_____

_____

_____

82. When I have a creative idea, am I able to see it through? How good am I at completion? How does it feel to complete a creative task? What seems to block me from completion? Do I run into mental or emotional stumbling blocks when exercising my creativity? If so, what are they? What can I do to mitigate their effects?

_____

_____

_____

_____

_____

_____

_____

_____

83. How do I nurture the creativity of those around me: my partner, children, colleagues, friends, etc.? Do I recognize their creative gifts? Am I good at supporting the creativity of others? If
so, how do I offer my support? If not, how might I become
more supportive?

_____

_____

_____

_____

_____

_____

84. Creativity and pleasure are related synergistically. Do I make
room in my life for pleasure? What do I do that is purely for fun
or pleasure? Where and when do I have the most fun or experience the most pleasure?

_____

_____

_____

85. With whom or where do I feel the most pleasure? What is pleasurable to me that no one else would consider to be so? What do
most people consider pleasurable that is not so for me?

♦ CHAPTER 7 ♦

Spiritual Life

Religion and spirituality are not necessarily the same thing. Although they may certainly travel the same path, there are certain characteristics that go beyond any specific religious beliefs and point to the spiritual nature we all share. The Hard Questions about spirituality, therefore, focus on those qualities that transcend organized religion. You can answer them whether or not you believe in God, the Goddess, Buddha, or all or none of the above. The Dalai Lama defined the difference most clearly in *Ethics for the New Millennium:* "Religion I take to be concerned with faith in the claims to salvation of one faith tradition or another . . . Connected with this are religious teachings or dogma, ritual, prayer, and so on. Spirituality I take to be concerned with those qualities of the human spirit—such as love and compassion, patience, tolerance, forgiveness, contentment, a sense of responsibility, a sense of harmony—which bring happiness to both self and others."

Spirituality is very often a quality in ourselves that we categorize as separate from the rest of our lives. Perhaps we go to church on Sundays or synagogue on the High Holy Days. Maybe we meditate for twenty minutes every day or seek a spiritual connection to the universe through hiking or making love or listening to music. And then, when we're not participating in these activities, we're unsure what to do with our spirituality until the next time we want or need to put it into practice. The questions in this chapter are intended to help you find ways to practice your spirituality every day, in everything you do. They ask you to examine not only your spiritual beliefs but also where and how those beliefs manifest at work, at home, and in relationships. They ask you to consider how your values, ethics, and core beliefs are reflected in your everyday actions and interactions.

Buddhists talk about three different spiritual paths, all valuable. The first is that of the monk or nun. This path involves renouncing the things of everyday life and living in a spiritual community. The second path is that of the hermit or so-called forest monk, one who goes into the woods or sits in a cave, determined to undertake spiritual practices in solitude until enlightenment is achieved. The third path is that of the "householder yogi," one who uses the stuff of everyday life—work, family, friends, even housekeeping and other chores—as his or her spiritual path. If you're reading this book, it's likely that you are already a householder yogi, even if you'd never have thought to call yourself one.

We're living in a very exciting spiritual time—a time when more and more of us are becoming householder yogis, people who want every aspect of their lives to have and support spiritual meaning, not just on the Sabbath, holy days, or holidays. While there are literally centuries of instruction for monks and hermits, there is relatively little instruction in any tradition for being a householder yogi, especially in modern times. It is, therefore, up to each of us to envision and define our own spiritual path, whether or not it involves church, synagogue, temple, liturgy, ritual, community, or even our family. The Hard Questions are meant to help you take the very beginning steps toward defining how, when, and where your spiritual nature is best expressed, regardless of your religious beliefs. They will help you to discover which spiritual qualities come easily to you and which seem more difficult. They will help you to determine whether your deepest spiritual beliefs and values are being reflected in the way you go about the business of your life. And, if not, what you might be able to do to eliminate that "disconnect" between your inner and outer lives.

As we all know, values and beliefs are continually evolving, deepening, disappearing, and reappearing. So of all the Hard Questions, these are probably the ones you will want to visit over and over again. In some sense, they are the most important questions of all. After you answer them, you may want to review your answers to questions in the earlier chapters to make sure they accurately reflect your spiritual values and beliefs.

86. What place do spirituality and spiritual practice play in my life? Do I have a spiritual life? Do I have spiritual beliefs? Are they the beliefs of a specific religion or are they self-created? A combination of the two? Am I able to express them clearly? To myself? To others?

_____

_____

_____

_____

_____

_____

_____

87. Do I believe in God or any form of deity? If so, what makes me feel most connected to this divinity? What is the nature of my relationship with this divinity? When do I feel it most strongly? Daily? In church? In nature? With my family? Others? What can I do to make this relationship stronger?

_____

_____

_____

_____

_____

_____

_____

88. Do I follow a particular spiritual practice or practices, such as meditation, prayer, charitable service? How strong is my commitment to these practices? Am I satisfied with the amount of time, energy, and resources I devote to them? If not, what changes might I make to deepen my practice?

_____

_____

_____

_____

_____

_____

89. Do I share my spiritual practice with others? If so, do I feel supported and am I able to offer support? If not, would I benefit from finding people to share my practice? How would I go about finding them?

_____

_____

_____

_____

_____

_____

_____

90. Does my family participate in my relationship with divinity? If so, am I content with the way we express and work with spirituality as a family? If not, would I like to try to strengthen the connection between my family life and my spiritual life?

_____

_____

_____

_____

_____

_____

91. What are the three qualities I value most? (For example, justice, generosity, honesty, equanimity, wisdom, faith, joy, power, love.) How deeply are these values expressed in my relationships with family, with an intimate partner, and in my work? Would my friends, family, partner, and colleagues be able to see my values expressed in my actions and interactions with them? How can I better express my core values in each important area of my life?

92. If I had to rank the areas of my life to reflect my deepest values and core inclinations, how would I order the following: family, friendships, intimacy, work, money, creativity, and spirituality? To which areas do I devote the most time, energy, resources, and thought? Am I content with this ranking? Would I prefer to reorder some of these priorities? If so, how might I go about doing that? Are internal and/or external shifts required? Who might be able to help me make those changes? Are there any books, groups, organizations, or friends I could call on for support? If my priorities were ordered correctly, how would my life be different from what it is now?

93. Which of my relationships are most supportive of my spiritual beliefs and values? With whom do I feel closest to God or divinity? Who is my best spiritual friend? With whom can I most comfortably discuss my beliefs and values? Which relationships best support me in my progress along my personal spiritual path? Which support me the least?

_____

_____

_____

_____

_____

_____

_____

94. How, where, and with whom do I most clearly express the spiritual qualities of love, compassion, patience, tolerance, forgiveness, contentment, and happiness? Which of these am I most lacking in? In which areas of my life and in which relationships? How can I cultivate and deepen these qualities in myself and in my everyday dealings with others?

_____

_____

_____

_____

_____

_____

_____

_____

95. Does the work I do support or reflect my spiritual beliefs and values? Is there congruity between how I believe we should treat others and my relationships at work? Do I feel good about the product, service, or aim of my workplace? If not, how might I bring my work life into closer alliance with my values? Is there some way I can "come from" my spiritual core while at work?

_____

_____

_____

_____

_____

_____

_____

96. For what and to whom am I most grateful in my life? What has been done for me or given to me that I am most appreciative of? What is currently being done for me or given to me that I'm most appreciative of? Am I able to express gratitude either through word or deed for what I've received and am receiving? How do I express gratitude?

_____

_____

_____

_____

_____

_____

_____

97. What do I do to be of service to others? Do I offer the fruits of my spiritual beliefs and practices to others? Do I give back to the world? Or am I simply not able to at this time? If I do express generosity, how do I do it? How might I increase the role of generosity in my life?

_____

_____

_____

_____

_____

_____

_____

_____

98. When someone is born or dies in my family or community, do I have a satisfactory way to mark these events? What rituals (formal or informal) help me to commemorate these major transitions?

_____

_____

_____

_____

_____

_____

_____

99. Do I celebrate or mourn any "spiritual events"? Which holidays or events (religious or personal) do I feel it is important to mark, either through celebration or remembrance/mourning? Do I have appropriate rituals and community to join or support me during these times?

_____

_____

100. What would I want to be written in my obituary or said about me in a eulogy?

AFTERWORD

Answering the Hard Questions need not—and in fact should not—be a "one time only" event. In fact, I believe in asking ourselves questions every day as a way to keep fine-tuning our ear to the sound of our inner voice. When you've answered all the Hard Questions, I therefore encourage you to use them (or any form of inquiry) daily as a way of staying connected with yourself.

I also encourage you to come up with a personalized list of questions that will help you to do that. Ask them in the morning to make sure your day is launched with consciousness. Or you can ask them in the evening as a way of reviewing, learning, and summarizing what really happened that day. You will feel listened to!

Here are some questions that work for me:

Start of day:

What do I need to say today? To whom?

With whom do I need to connect today?

What would I like to see unfold in my life today?

What can I contribute today? To whom? To what?

What can I focus on today that will bring me closer to my authentic life?

End of day:

What did I leave unsaid today?

What did I allow myself to feel?

What didn't I allow myself to feel?

What did I love about myself today? What did I not love about myself today?

What began to unfold in my life today?

What happened today for which am I grateful?

What happened today that wasn't in accord with my highest values?

What did I say, do, think, or feel today that brought me closer to my authentic life?

It may take some effort to answer these questions, but eventually dialoging with yourself in this way can help you to develop the habit of inner awareness. This habit—the ability to be present to your own life—is the best way to find your own answers, the real answers, the answers that can best serve you and those around you.

We shall not cease from exploration
And the end of all our exploring
Will be to arrive where we started
And know the place for the first time.
—T.S. Eliot, *Little Gidding*

To learn more about answering the Hard Questions, visit *www.thehardquestions.com*.